Natasha Mac a'Bháird is a writer and editor. She is
the author of the bestselling book *The Irish Bride's
Survival Guide* and of seven books for children.
Natasha lives in Dublin with her family.

The Irish Bridesmaid's GUIDE

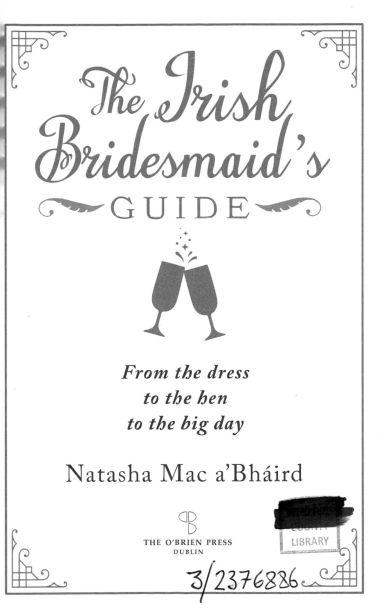

*From the dress
to the hen
to the big day*

Natasha Mac a'Bháird

THE O'BRIEN PRESS
DUBLIN

First published 2019 by
The O'Brien Press Ltd,
12 Terenure Road East, Rathgar,
Dublin 6, Ireland.
Tel: +353 1 4923333; Fax: +353 1 4922777
E-mail: books@obrien.ie.
Website: www.obrien.ie
The O'Brien Press is a member of Publishing Ireland.

ISBN: 978-1-78849-044-3

8 7 6 5 4 3 2 1
23 22 21 20 19

Printed and bound in Poland by Białostockie Zakłady Graficzne S.A.
The paper in this book is produced using pulp from managed forests.

Published in

DUBLIN
UNESCO
City of Literature

Table of Contents

Dedication
To my fabulous bridesmaids,
Áine, Catherine and Louise

Acknowledgements
Thank you to all the brides and bridesmaids
who were kind enough to share their experiences
with me – this book wouldn't be the same without
you. Thank you to the staff at The O'Brien Press,
especially my editor, Nicola Reddy, for tons of
fantastic ideas and an eagle eye. Thank you to
Aidan, Rachel and Sarah for reading early drafts,
helping me find the perfect quotes,
and for everything.

~ Introduction ~

$\mathcal{C}$ongratulations – you've been asked to be a bridesmaid! Your friend or sister is planning the most important day of her life and she wants you to be a special part of it – what could be nicer than that? You're in for a lot of fun, laughter and happy times as you help her make memories she'll treasure for the rest of her life.

But once the initial thrill of being chosen for this honour wears off, you might be wondering what you've let yourself in for! How much is expected of you, and how can you be the fabulous bridesmaid your lovely friend deserves? Never fear, you've made the best start by picking up this book, which will guide you through this exciting, fun-filled and, yes, occasionally stressful time.

First things first: What kind of bridesmaid are you, and what does the role involve?

'My Way': Chief bridesmaid

You're the chosen one – the one the bride is going to rely on for everything, and you'll organise the rest of the bridesmaids. It's quite a responsibility. But you also have the honour of knowing you're the one she trusts the most and wants right by her side on her big day.

'Me & My Girls': One of the bridesmaid gang

Easy peasy, right? You get all the fun of the celebrations, the dress, the flowers, without too much of the responsibility. But don't relax and kick off those heels just yet – you still have an important role to play. And maybe you could help take some of the pressure off the chief bridesmaid by taking care of one particular job? More on this later.

'The One and Only': Solo bridesmaid

Wow – that's quite an honour, and also something of a burden. With no one else to share the planning, it's all down to you whether things run smoothly. On the other hand, you don't need to worry about fitting in

A QUICK GUIDE TO THE BRIDESMAID'S ROLE

As a bridesmaid, you may be called upon to perform any or all of these tasks:

- Help the bride to choose her wedding dress
- Help to choose your own dress and dresses for the other bridesmaids and flower girls
- Plan the hen party (in consultation with the bride)
- Attend the wedding rehearsal
- Stay with the bride the night before the wedding
- Help the bride get ready on the morning of the wedding
- Be at the venue when the bride arrives and check that everything is perfect before she walks down the aisle
- Keep an eye on any children in the wedding party (flower girls, page boys, ring bearers)
- Hold the bride's bouquet during the ceremony
- Stand with the bride and groom during the vows
- Sign the register as official witness to the marriage (usually the job of the chief bridesmaid)
- Accompany the best man or a groomsman up the aisle
- Be available to run errands or deal with any problems that arise at the reception
- Make a speech at the reception

with other bridesmaids' fashion tastes, you can make quick decisions without having to consult anyone else, and the glory of knowing how well the hen party went will be all yours!

> *'Of all possessions a friend is the most precious.'*
> — *Herodotus*

CHAPTER ONE

What Does the Bridesmaid Do?

So now that you've accepted the role of bridesmaid, you're probably wondering what's going to be expected of you in the lead-up to the wedding. Obviously your number-one priority is to be there for the bride on the day, looking fabulous and drinking champagne, but there's a little more to it than that. In the Introduction we saw the duties traditionally expected of the bridesmaid. But those are really just the basics, and with weddings becoming more elaborate and brides more invested in the perfect day, you might find yourself having to perform some or all of the following roles over the next few months.

Personal shopper

The bride is going to be spending quite sizeable chunks of her life parading up and down shop floors in dresses of varying shades of white. Who better to stand there admiring her and offering tactful opinions than her bridesmaid? There's quite often a glass of prosecco in it for you, too.

Fashion expert

Let's not forget your own dress. Once the bride's dress is sorted, if you can get out there and do some window shopping for the perfect bridesmaid dress, you may be able to save the bride a lot of work. There's the added bonus that you're more likely to get a dress that's to your taste … but of course that's not your main motivation, right?

Social coordinator

You'll need to organise things with the other bridesmaids, especially if you're the chief bridesmaid. If you've ever gone away with a group of friends, you'll have some idea of how tricky it can be to coordinate plans to suit everyone. Lots of patience and a firm hand are required here.

Party planner

The hen party looms large. All the most important women in the bride's life will be getting together to help her wave goodbye to her single life in style. And you're in charge of organising this once-in-a-lifetime celebration. No pressure or anything …

Therapist

Even the calmest bride can get a little overwhelmed by all the smaller details that go into planning a wedding – not to mention the pressure of trying to keep everyone happy. Be prepared for a meltdown at some point, and trust that your calm reassurance will be enough to soothe her troubled spirits.

General dogsbody

One of the ways you can help the bride is to simply take over some of her jobs. Booking hair appointments, calling suppliers to confirm details, collecting dresses from the dressmaker – little things that won't take up too much of your time, but might make all the difference to a stressed bride.

Pre-marriage counsellor

Hopefully this role won't be called on, but if her future husband is wrecking the bride's head then your shoulder is likely to be the one she cries on. Bring tissues. And chocolate.

BEST BRIDESMAID EVER

Do you have fabulous design skills that could be put to use designing invitations, wedding booklets and other stationery? Could you bake the wedding cake, plan the music or do the bridal party's make-up? Do you run a business or own a property that could make for a truly original hen party? This could be the perfect way to contribute to the bride's big day and ensure you go down in bridesmaid history. Don't set the bar too high, though, unless you're prepared to follow through – you'll have a lot to live up to as the wedding plans unfold (not to mention making all the less fabulous bridesmaids hate you).

'In the sweetness of friendship let there be laughter,
and sharing of pleasures. For in the dew of little things
the heart finds its morning and is refreshed.'
— *Kahlil Gibran,* **The Prophet**

What's in a name?

You might find that any or all of these terms crop up, so it's good to know what is meant by each.

Chief bridesmaid/maid of honour/ matron of honour

The chief bridesmaid is the bride's right-hand woman, go-to girl, you get the picture. Also known as maid of honour (particularly in America) or matron of honour if she is married, though this is a particularly hideous term which conjures up images of a school matron dressed in starchy white with a face like thunder. So we'll stick with chief bridesmaid for now, thank you very much. **Inspo:** Katherine Heigl's uber-dedicated Jane in *27 Dresses*

Bridesmaid

If you are an ordinary bridesmaid, with a chief brides-maid ranking above you, then you get all the fun and a bit less of the responsibility (and the glory, but that's not why you're there, right?). **Inspo:** The gang from *Bridesmaids*

Junior bridesmaid

Sometimes a girl aged around 10–15 – perhaps a daughter or niece of the bride – might be asked to be a junior bridesmaid. This is a nice way of making them feel part of the wedding without placing too many demands on them. It's up to the bride whether they wear the same style of dress as the older bridesmaids or something different. They can stand with the bridal party for the ceremony. **Inspo:** Cher Horowitz (Alicia Silverstone) in bubblegum pink at the end of *Clueless*

Flower girl

Younger girls who the bride wishes to include can be flower girls. Their dresses are usually the same colour as the bride's rather than the bridesmaids'. They walk down the aisle with the bridal party, possibly carrying flowers or scattering petals, but they don't need to stand during the ceremony. Actually, their main role is to look cute for the photos. **Inspo:** Princess Charlotte (who is basically a professional flower girl at this stage)

Best woman

This term usually applies to a female friend or sister of the groom whom he has asked to be his closest attendant, instead of a best man. But if you're the bride's right-hand woman and you both prefer the name 'best woman' to the traditional 'bridesmaid', then there's no reason you can't use it too! **Inspo:** The bestest of them all, Pippa Middleton

Bridesman

A male friend or brother of the bride who's part of the bride's attendants rather than the groom's (his would be called a groomsman). **Inspo:** Ryan Seacrest, who cried giving the Man of Honour speech at his sister's wedding (aww!)

Getting to know the other bridesmaids

If the bride is having three or four bridesmaids, chances are you might not all know each other well. Maybe she's having her sister, the groom's sister, her best friend from school, and her closest work colleague. Organise an outing so you can all get to know each other a little – a Sunday brunch or meeting for a drink on a Friday evening would be the perfect way to break the ice.

Let everyone introduce themselves, saying a few words about how they know the bride. But be careful – don't say 'I'm Mary's closest friend, she tells me everything'. Maybe your fellow bridesmaid, who has known Mary since they bonded over a mutual love of eating the Play-Doh at toddler group, thinks that's her role. Remember – it's not a competition.

If you're feeling a bit shy about having to make conversation with a group of strangers, focus on what you have in common: the bride. Asking people questions is a good conversation starter. What did they think of the way John proposed? Have they been to the wedding venue before? Have they got any good ideas for the hen party? But try to steer clear of controversial subjects – you don't want your very first meet-up to end on a sour note.

It's a good idea, even at this early stage, to start planning who's going to take care of what – taking the bride's wishes into account, of course. It's usually the chief bridesmaid's job to plan the hen party, but maybe one of the other bridesmaids would be more suitable. If she's a professional party planner – or is so skilled at this that she might as well be – it would be crazy not to take advantage of her experience. Does another bridesmaid have some expertise in a different area that would come in useful? Now is the time to start gathering that information and divvying up tasks.

'Kindred spirits are not so scarce as I used to think. It's splendid to find there are so many of them in the world.'
— *L.M. Montgomery,* **Anne of Green Gables**

17

Staying in touch

Decide on the best way to communicate with one another, and make sure no one is going to be left out. A WhatsApp or private Facebook group is probably a better idea than email, where important information is more likely to get drowned in a long list of Reply All's.

Be selective in what you share with the group. A few dress suggestions is fine, but a constant barrage of photos might make people tune out, and then you won't get replies to important queries.

Keep messages short and to the point (without being too business-like, of course!), and make it clear when you need an answer by. 'If you could let me know by Friday what your preference is, I'll make the booking then.' And don't shoot down someone else's suggestion unless you're prepared to put the effort in to find an alternative. There's nothing more frustrating in these situations than someone who says no to everyone else's suggestions but can't seem to be bothered coming up with their own.

'We're all a little weird. And life is a little weird. And when we find someone whose weirdness is compatible with ours, we join up with them and fall into mutually satisfying weirdness – and call it love – true love.'
— *Robert Fulghum,* True Love

Bridesmaid types

Have you spotted any of these among your fellow bridesmaids? As the old saying goes, forewarned is forearmed, so you can think about the best way to handle them. And if you can't spot any of them – maybe it's you?

The Flake

She's so sorry she had to cancel your coffee date to discuss the dresses, but she just remembered she had a thing. But she's absolutely going to book the restaurant for the hen party, right after she finishes checking out the options – she might try one her boyfriend mentioned, and she's sure she read a review of that new place, she just needs to remember what it's called. But she's going to get to it, any second now. What do you mean, you really need to book a restaurant for twenty people more than a couple of days in advance?

How to deal: Don't trust her with anything important. It'll be a lot less hassle if you do it yourself!

The Know-It-All

If she was getting married, she wouldn't have it in this hotel – it's so common, and she thinks it's so important that weddings are unique, don't you? And that band the bride has chosen are so last year. As for the dress, well, she doesn't want to say anything to the bride, but white really isn't her colour, is it?

How to deal: Smile and nod and tell her firmly that you're sure the bride's wedding is going to be just as special as she is.

The Reluctant One

She's always the last one to answer emails (if she answers them at all), never seems to have time to get together for any shopping or planning, and when you do manage to get hold of her, her answer to every suggestion is 'Whatever'.

How to deal: Avoid bombarding her with information and questions, and just leave her out of the smaller questions. Maybe she genuinely has a lot going on in her life that means she can't embrace the wedding celebrations as wholeheartedly as you can. But if her lack of enthusiasm is upsetting the bride, have a quiet word about getting her act together – after all, you know the bride would do the same for her.

The Boss

There's no point in coming up with suggestions about the colour of the dresses or the venue for the hen party, because this bridesmaid is already completely convinced her way is the only way. In fact she'd be quite happy to take over the actual wedding planning, if only the bride and groom didn't insist on having opinions of their own.

How to deal: A little bit of flattery might be the best way to handle this tricky bridesmaid – 'Those are great ideas! Let's put everyone's suggestions together and see if we can come up with something the bride will really love' – before gently steering her in a different direction. But if she's not open to subtlety, remind her that it's not actually all up to her, given that there's this person called the bride to consider.

The Rebel

Her purple hair is clashing with the powder-blue dresses, she wouldn't dream of covering up her tattoos and you definitely don't fancy the job of prising her out of her Doc Marten boots.

How to deal: Before you get too uptight, ask yourself: How important is any of this to the bride? Maybe she's a relaxed bride who wants everyone to just be themselves and enjoy the day. However, if she's having a very formal, traditional wedding and would prefer her friend not to stick out a mile, she might appreciate you suggesting that The Rebel at least skip the black lipstick for the day.

The Skint One

She heaves a huge sigh of relief when the bride

makes it clear she's paying for the dresses. When another bridesmaid suggests afternoon tea in the Merrion, she puts forward a picnic in the park as an alternative, or else mutters something about possibly being busy that day.

How to deal: It's not her fault she's broke, so do be sympathetic. Try to keep costs down as much as you can and offer alternatives where possible – lots of tips on this later. Where costs are unavoidable, try to plan them well in advance so she can at least budget for it. And if you think the bride is unaware of the situation, mention it discreetly so the broke bridesmaid doesn't feel under too much pressure.

The tradition of having bridesmaids dates from pagan times. Bridesmaids wore the same dress as the bride in order to confuse evil spirits who might want to ruin her happiness!

CHAPTER TWO

The Dress

*C*hoosing the bridesmaid dress should be a fun opportunity for girl bonding and giggles. Of course, if you're dealing with a Bridezilla who has her mind firmly made up and couldn't care less about your wishes, it also has the potential to turn into the shopping trip from hell. For now let's assume yours is a lovely bride who has your best interests at heart (more on coping with the other kind later).

The choice of bridesmaid dress is, of course, ultimately up to the bride. It needs to fit in with the style of the wedding, and with her own dress in particular. When it comes to colour, the bridesmaid dress is usually the main colour of the wedding. Flowers, stationery and decorations will all need to fit in with it, so there's not a lot of room for manoeuvre here if the bride has a vision.

This doesn't mean you should resign yourself to having no say in your dress. In fact you have plenty of potential to influence the bride – and the best way to do this is to get in early with your suggestions. It's a lot easier to subtly steer the bride in a direction of your choosing from the start, rather than trying to talk her out of something she has her heart set on.

If you have been helping the bride with the wedding plans – and especially if you've gone shopping for her dress with her – then you probably have a good idea of the style of dress that will suit the wedding. If you know the colour, or possible colours, that the bride is thinking of, then why not have a look online and see if you can find some potential winners. The bride will probably be grateful that you've helped narrow down her search, and at the same time you'll let her know your own preferences. Win win!

'True friends are like diamonds: bright, beautiful, valuable and always in style.'— Nicole Richie

When to shop

It's really up to the bride to let you know when she wants to go shopping for the bridesmaid dresses, but if you're the planning-ahead sort, then you might want to know that six to twelve months before the wedding is a good general guideline.

For a more formal, traditional wedding where the bride wants bridesmaid dresses from a specialised boutique, you will need to order these well in advance – at least six months before the wedding. If you're buying off the peg, it can be left until a bit later. For online shopping, it's a good idea to allow plenty of time for shipping, and for returning items if it turns out they're not a success.

Basically, there's absolutely no reason not to get this job out of the way early – then you can relax and look forward to the glamorous vision you will present on the day.

The bride will need to have her own dress chosen first so the styles complement each other. If she is going for a full-on traditional white meringue, then the sleek little cocktail number you had in mind is unlikely to cut it, unfortunately.

Where to shop

To keep things simple, the bride might want to start with the bridal boutique where she's getting her own dress. But you may well find yourselves doing a tour of all the bridal boutiques in town – and beyond – in search of the perfect bridesmaid dress.

More and more brides are choosing bridesmaid dresses that aren't from a bridal boutique or range at all. So you could well end up with something that you can wear again, instead of leaving it to languish in the back of your wardrobe. But do bear in mind that if you're going for a dress from a high street

'Friendship isn't about who you've known the longest.
It's about who walked into your life, said
"I'm here for you" and proved it.'
— Author unknown

store, there's a greater chance of another wedding guest turning up in the same frock, especially if you've bought it close to the wedding.

It might be a good idea – with the bride's permission of course – to quietly spread the word that guests should avoid a particular colour. No one wants to turn up at the wedding looking like a wannabe bridesmaid.

Shopping strategies

If there are lots of bridesmaids, it's a good idea for the bride and the chief bridesmaid to go on an initial recce to get a sense of what's out there, what fits in with the style of the wedding, and what you like. Don't make a final decision, though, until everyone has seen the dress you have in mind – or ideally a small range of options.

'Love is but the discovery of ourselves in others, and the delight in the recognition.'
— Alexander Smith

What to wear when dress shopping

Wear **comfortable clothes** that you can change out of easily – this is going to be a long day. It definitely helps to wear **heels** with the dress to get a proper sense of how it will look. If you can't bear the thought of trekking around town in heels, just bring a pair with you that you can slip on in the shop. And if you have a **strapless bra,** wear that too – it will give you a better picture of what the dress looks like than if you're trying to squish bra straps under your armpits while checking yourself out in the mirror.

Don't go shopping when you're horribly hungover. It will be hell, and nothing will look good on you. You have been warned!

Wear a bit of **make-up**, but not so much fake tan that the shop assistant panics when she sees you coming. It'll help if you're looking your best. If you have long hair that you plan to wear up for the wedding, put it up or just into a **ponytail** – it can really affect how the neckline of the dress looks on you.

When you're trying a dress on, don't just look at it in the mirror. Walk around the shop to make sure it feels

THE IRISH BRIDESMAID'S GUIDE

comfortable to move in. Try sitting down in it too, and take photos on your phone. Be honest with the bride if it's really not working. There are other alternatives out there that will still blend in with her theme.

How much say do I really have?

If you really hate the chosen **colour** and feel it doesn't suit you at all, you have a bit of a dilemma. You know your bride best: Is she the laidback type who doesn't really care about the colour scheme as long as everyone is happy? Or does she have a very clear vision of a perfectly coordinated wedding where eclectic just won't cut it? If it's the latter, be prepared to just suck it up. It's only one day out of your life.

Where you do have a bit more leeway is in the **style** of the dress. The bride might have a strapless gown in mind, but if you hate revealing that much flesh, there's nothing wrong with steering her gently in the direction of something more covered up. And if dresses with a straight line are clinging to lumps and bumps you'd really rather not draw attention to, it's

30

A QUICK GUIDE TO DRESS STYLES

- **Ballgown:** A classic princess style with a fitted waist and a skirt with tons of volume. ***Best for:*** Traditional weddings and most body shapes, though very short bridesmaids may look a little swamped.

- **A-line:** A similar shape to a ballgown but with much less material. ***Best for:*** A classic look that's flattering for all body shapes.

- **Mermaid:** A style that clings to all your curves and flares out at the bottom for that mermaid or fishtail look. ***Best for:*** Showing off your figure, especially if you've got a Kardashian bum.

- **Empire:** Fitted under the bust to fall in flattering folds around the waist and hips. ***Best for:*** Ideal if you're a bit self-conscious about your tummy – and perfect for pregnant bridesmaids!

- **Sheath:** A straight, fitted dress, usually in clingy material. ***Best for:*** Tall, willowy figures will carry this style best (though there's always magic underwear …).

absolutely fine to suggest a more flattering style. With so much out there to choose from – not to mention the option of getting dresses made to order – it should be possible to find a compromise that you, the bride and the other bridesmaids will be happy with.

Finding it hard to suit everyone?

Bridesmaids come in all different shapes, sizes and colouring. The same dress might suit everyone – but then again, it might not. If you're having issues, there are ways around this:

- Get a dress made up using the same fabric but in different styles.
- Have the same dress in two different colours, or for three or more bridesmaids go for a range of colours within the same palette.
- Go for the eclectic option – search online for 'mix and match' bridesmaid dresses to get some ideas. Just make sure that whatever you go for works as an ensemble, rather than looking like you all rocked up in whatever the hell you felt like.

'My sister had four bridesmaids, and we all had very different shapes and senses of style. She knew it would be impossible to find one dress we'd all feel comfortable in, so she bought the fabric she wanted and gave us free rein to have it made up in whatever style of dress we wanted. It was lovely to see the different options everyone came up with – one strapless with an A-line skirt, one empire line, one off the shoulder and straight and one with cap sleeves – and it made for a real talking point on the day.'

Rebecca, bridesmaid

Size does matter

Don't be tempted to order a dress in a smaller size with the idea of losing weight before the wedding. You're just putting a ton of unnecessary pressure on yourself at what's already a busy and stressful time. If you do need to lose weight then the wedding might be the goal that will help you along the way, but you should order the dress in the size you are now. It's much easier to take in a dress that's too big than to let out one that's too small. That's a headache you don't want the week before the wedding.

What if you're secretly pregnant and don't want to tell the bride yet? Check out p75 for tips!

'I lost six stone to be a bridesmaid. I was a size 14–16. The dressmaker ordered me a size 26, and all the seams had to be taken in eight inches. She then made it too small! I spent a week in Cuba in a gym without air conditioning, trying to fit into the dress!'

Vicky, bridesmaid

Online shopping

Buying the bridesmaid dresses online can be a great way to save time and money. Just make sure you allow plenty of time to exchange the dresses if it doesn't work out, and check the company's returns policy and the cost of return shipping. Although you'll miss out on the girly bonding of a shopping trip, you can still make it into a special occasion.

'My sister ordered three different dresses for me and the other bridesmaid to try on. As I had a young toddler and my husband was away for the weekend, we got together in my house. My son loved watching us try the dresses on! Thankfully we both liked the same one. It was brilliant having it at home – I was able to put my son to bed and then enjoy the celebrations with a cheese board, chocolates and a couple of bottles of bubbly.' *Jane, bridesmaid*

What do I have to pay for?

The good news is that it's traditional in Ireland for the bride and groom to pay for the bridesmaid dresses. So if she's forcing you to wear something hideous, spare a thought for the unlucky American bridesmaid who's not only wearing an ugly dress but having to bankrupt herself for the privilege!

If you know the bride and groom are really strapped for cash, and if she's being kind enough to let you choose your own dress, then it would be a nice gesture to offer to pay for it yourself – after all, you'll have the freedom to choose something you can wear again. Another option might be for the bride to sell the dresses afterwards as a set.

'I had quite a traditional wedding with long pink gowns that I knew the three bridesmaids wouldn't wear again. I sold them on afterwards and the four of us had a night out with the money!' *Eleanor, bride*

Shoes

Make sure you go shopping for shoes in the afternoon, as your feet can really swell as the day goes on. Beware of stiletto heels if you're expecting to spend a lot of the day outdoors – getting stuck in the hotel's front lawn could really ruin that photo shoot. Try to resist the temptation to buy shoes that look fabulous but feel really uncomfortable. You're going to be **on your feet** for most of the day – and night! If you really can't resist those killer heels then think about bringing a pair of flats to change into for **dancing**.

If the bride is insisting that all the bridesmaids should wear **specific shoes** to match the dress, then she should be the one to pay. If on the other hand something more **generic** will do the trick – nude high heels, silver sandals – then you could offer to pay for them yourself, or even suggest that you wear something you already own.

Be sure to **break in** your shoes by wearing them around the house for an hour here and there before the wedding day. Make sure the **soles** aren't slippery, too. You don't want to go flying down that highly polished church aisle! You can give them more grip by scuffing them up a bit on concrete.

> *'To get the full value of joy you must have*
> *someone to divide it with.'*
> — *Mark Twain*

What else do I need?

You might want to think about a **wrap** to wear over your dress, or maybe a faux fur **cape** for a winter wedding, but check what the bride has in mind. If she wants you to wear particular **hair accessories**, she will probably provide them, and bridesmaids often find themselves presented with a pretty **necklace** as a thank you – but do be ready with your own in case this isn't part of the bride's plans.

Don't underestimate the power of the right **underwear** to transform your look! If you don't already own a high-quality strapless or convertible bra, it's well worth your while investing in one – and unlike the dress, you will definitely wear it again. And slimming underwear or **tights** can give you a real confidence boost; just make sure they're comfortable.

Don't forget to plan the **handbag** too (as well as whatever bag you might want to bring with emergency supplies for the bride – more on that later).

'If the wedding is in winter make sure the bridesmaid has something warm to wear over her dress, not just the bride. I was lovely and snug at my December wedding but my poor sister was freezing in her strapless dress because we forgot about her! I had to steal a pashmina, jacket and hat from a guest.' *Beth, bride*

What if the bride is trying to force the dress from hell on you?

It's acres of peach taffeta. It's a high-necked, long-sleeved gingham frock that might have looked good on a four-year-old in 1972. It's a black leather mini-skirted number with a neckline that is guaranteed to make the priest's eyeballs pop out of their sockets. Whatever the particular form of hideousness she's trying to insist you wear, your gentle hints and lack of enthusiasm are getting you nowhere. This is an extreme situation, and extreme measures are called for.

What are the reasons behind the bride's choice of this particular dress? Is her fashion sense genuinely that bad, or could she possibly be trying to ensure there's no chance of her bridesmaid outshining her?

Either way, this may be a good time to introduce some wedding anecdotes that might persuade her to change her mind. For example:

'This bride I know picked the most ridiculous-looking dresses for the bridesmaids. At the ceremony, it was all anyone could talk about – no one even noticed what the bride was wearing.'

'Have you ever noticed that when the bridesmaid dresses are simple and classy, the bride's dress really stands out?'

'When my friend was a bridesmaid, her dress was so uncomfortable she just couldn't relax all day. You can really tell from her expression in the wedding photos – it just put a downer on the whole day.'

These stories should be enough to strike fear into the heart of any sensible bride-to-be. But if all else fails, point out to her that while she and her beloved are the beautiful portrait everyone has come to admire, they won't be able to concentrate on it if it's surrounded by an ugly frame!

'My sister-in-law asked me to be bridesmaid when I was six months pregnant. She'd already bought the dresses a year before. Obviously mine didn't fit so she paid someone (a friend, not a dressmaker) to make a replica that would fit over my bump. She paid the deposit and bought all the material before asking me. I was too polite to say no and ended up wearing a dress that looked like a sack. Even the photographer said "Wow – you're a kind bridesmaid wearing that!" The bride was surprised (and offended) when I got changed for the evening do. I thought I was being exceedingly nice wearing the dress/sack for the group photos.' *Fiona, bridesmaid*

BEST BRIDESMAID EVER

Amidst all the strapless bras, pushy sales staff, tired feet and differing opinions, don't forget to make dress shopping special for the bride. This is an exciting time in her life that she won't have back – it's worth making an occasion of it. Why not meet for brunch before going shopping, or celebrate afterwards with afternoon tea or cocktails? Or if funds are an issue, invite everyone back to yours for something more low-key. Either way, it will ensure the day is one that the bride remembers for the right reasons.

CHAPTER THREE

The Hen Party

*N*ow to what is undoubtedly your biggest bridesmaid responsibility before the wedding day itself: That's right, organising the hen party. The joyous coming together of all the important women in the bride's life, in a riot of feather boas, L-plates, high heels and champagne, for this last hurrah before you wave her off into married life with a flourish. Scared yet?

From the moment you were asked to be bridesmaid, you've either been relishing the prospect, gleefully coming up with ideas about how you can give the bride a fantastic send-off, or else you've been absolutely dreading being in charge of a night's (or a weekend's) entertainment for a rowdy gang of women who'll be expecting you to pull out all the stops.

Fear not – whichever type of bridesmaid you are, there are plenty of ways to maximise the fun and minimise the stress.

Know your bride

Does the thought of falling out of a nightclub in the wee hours, veil askew and L-plates flying, and stumbling home still singing songs sound like her perfect night out – or fill her with horror? Would she consider afternoon tea to be classy and sophisticated – or as dull as watching paint dry? Don't get too invested in a type of celebration that's just not her thing. And what if she's saying she doesn't want a hen party at all? See p70 for how to deal.

Know your group

While the bride may be on for a glitzy weekend in Las Vegas, downing champagne and spinning the roulette wheel with gay abandon, her friends might have budget issues, travel plans of their own, small children, or simply an aversion to slot machines. There's not much point in ploughing all your time and effort into an event no one except yourself and the bride will be interested in attending.

The best starting point is to discuss with the bride who she wants to invite, as this will have a bearing on the type of party that will work. Is it a smaller group of close friends her own age, or a larger group including work colleagues, mothers and aunts? Will it be all girls or are the boys invited too? Come up with a guest list and think about what sort of activities and entertainment would be most enjoyable for everyone – remembering of course that the bride's wishes come first!

Ask the bride for the contact details of everyone she wants to invite and make a plan for how you will keep them updated on the plans – email, WhatsApp, Facebook, etc. – bearing in mind that if it's a large group of mixed ages you're bound to have one or two social media refusers who you'll need to contact separately.

Do I have to organise the hen party?

If you're the chief bridesmaid, the hen party is generally your responsibility. But sometimes this might be difficult for you – maybe you're living abroad or are very busy with your career or small children. Or maybe it's just that you find the idea of all the organisation it demands – researching ideas, coordinating schedules, liaising with venues – a little overwhelming.

You can choose to step outside your comfort zone and just do it. You can find a way to keep it as low-key as possible. Or, if you really must, you can opt out. Maybe another bridesmaid would be happy to take over, or even the bride herself – after all, she's the one who knows all the guests, and who knows best what she wants!

Whatever your reason, if you do feel that organising the hen party is beyond you, make that call as early as possible, and talk to the bride. The last thing you want is to add to her stress when she has so much on her plate.

> *'When sisters stand shoulder to shoulder,*
> *who stands a chance against us?'*
> — *Pam Brown*

Setting a date

A month or two before the wedding is a good time to hold the hen party – close enough to the big day that the excitement will be mounting, but far enough away that it won't impact on the final wedding preparations. Weekends are precious and the bride and groom will have things they need to do together close to the date. You might want to coordinate the hen with the groom's stag party, especially if you're planning to hold all or part of it in the home they share.

Don't be tempted to hold the hen party the night before the wedding, even if it seems like the ideal option as everyone will be in town. On the eve of her wedding the bride shouldn't have anything on her schedule beyond relaxing with those closest to her, having a long soak in a bubble bath, and getting an early night.

If you are expecting a huge group to attend the hen party, don't get too bogged down in trying to find a date that suits everyone – it's impossible. Consult the bride (obviously), the other bridesmaids, and anyone else the bride especially wants to include – maybe a sister who isn't in the bridal party, or a friend who lives overseas and can only travel on certain dates. Then just pick a date and ask everyone to put it in their diaries.

Making plans

Ask the bride how much she wants to be involved in the plans. Maybe she has some specific ideas in mind – on the other hand, maybe she's happy to leave it all to you! It's nice to have at least some element of surprise for her. Make sure you know if there is anything the bride definitely does or does NOT want. She will probably have been to several other hen parties before, so a good way to get started is to ask her what she liked about them (and what she hated).

Talk to the other bridesmaids about what you've got planned, and do listen if they're worried that it won't be to the bride's taste. You all know the bride from different times in her life and in different ways, so brainstorming ideas may well prove effective.

'I really hate tacky hen party stuff and had told my bridesmaids I didn't want it. So I was mortified when they produced willy straws and an edible thong – especially since it was in front of my grandmother and my very prudish mother-in-law-to-be! I got my fiancé to pick me up early and cried all the way home.' ***Ciara, bride***

Who pays?

Everyone should pay for themselves and chip in a bit extra for the bride. If you're going abroad or doing something else fairly pricey, then covering the bride's dinner and drinks is enough – don't feel obliged to subsidise her five-star accommodation.

If you are making a group booking for a hotel or service provider which requires payment in advance, let all the hens know you will need a deposit by a certain date. If some of the hens keep making excuses or simply not responding to you, make it clear that you can't reserve a place for them until you get their deposit. With so many options for sending money nowadays, such as PayPal or a transfer via internet banking, there's no need for people to keep you waiting.

Depending on where you're staying, it might make sense to let everyone make their own hotel reservations. Give them the name and contact details for the hotel and leave it up to them – that way you won't have to worry about chasing up last-minute absentees or being stuck with an enormous credit card bill.

Booking venues and people

Do your research. Don't pick a restaurant because some blogger said it's cool – go there yourself and try it out, if at all possible, or get a personal recommendation. Looking trendy on your Facebook check-in isn't going to be much good if the chicken wings are cold or the waiting staff are rubbish! If you're hiring someone – a make-up artist to give you a lesson, an astrologer to do everyone's birth charts, or even a stripper – make sure you read all their reviews online, if you can't meet them in person. You could also talk to them on the phone just to make sure you get a good vibe.

So what kind of hen party is it to be?

Will it be a typical hen party, involving dinner, drinks and general debauchery, either at home or away? Something wild and extravagant, or relaxed and low-key? There are so many options you can consider, so don't be afraid to let your imagination run wild!

'My sister-in-law had two hen weekends. The first was for family and in-laws – we stayed the night in a beautiful boutique hotel, had afternoon tea, did a cookery class together and had a lovely meal in the evening and breakfast the next day. She then had a much more raucous weekend in Cardiff with her school and college friends, which was lots of fun but which older family members would not have enjoyed! Having two meant she got the best of both worlds and no one felt uncomfortable.'

Joanne, bridesmaid

City break abroad

The lure of a trip abroad is easy to understand – strolling through the streets of Paris checking out the latest fashions, sipping cocktails at sunset in a piazza in Rome, soaking up the sun in Málaga, or dancing the night away in a trendy London night-club. There are so many cities just a short flight away where you can be sure of a few days of sightseeing, shopping, fine dining and fabulous nightlife. It's hard to beat a weekend away with the girls, with the usual day-to-day chores and responsibilities left far behind.

You can keep costs down by booking flights well in advance and choosing self-catering via Airbnb or similar, rather than a hotel. But whatever you do it's not going to be a cheap option, and it is bound to be more difficult for some people to attend, so do bear that in mind.

So where will you go? Is there somewhere you know the bride would love to visit, especially if it's a destination best suited to a gang of girls rather than a romantic break with her beloved? Try to choose somewhere that doesn't involve long flights or transfer times. Why waste time sitting on a bus when you could be getting started on those cocktails?

Plan some fun things to do when you get there,

and do make a reservation for dinner. But don't try to timetable every hour – half the fun of visiting somewhere new is just wandering around and discovering the sights for yourself.

Weekend away in Ireland

This option should work out cheaper than going abroad and will give people more flexibility over travel arrangements. If one of the hens can't miss work on Friday, they can travel to join you afterwards; or if another doesn't want to leave her children for two nights, she might be able to manage just the Saturday. Carrick-on-Shannon, Kilkenny and Letterkenny are all popular destinations. Just make sure the restaurant or other venue is happy to accommodate hens, as some aren't keen.

You could also consider a spa weekend. Relaxing massages, mud facials, body scrubs, all in the company of a great group of females, could prove the perfect way to make the bride's wedding stress disappear and leave you all looking and feeling fabulous just in time for the wedding.

Hen parties at home

There are many upsides to having a hen party at home: You can bond better as a gang without the distraction of bright lights and pub noise (not to mention the stag parties trying to chat you up!). It can be the perfect option if the budget is an issue, or if the bride hates the thought of being the focus of attention as she goes around the town. And staying in is the new going out, after all.

Slumber Party: Let's face it, this was pretty much every young girl's favourite way to get together with her besties. Now that you're older and (slightly) wiser, there's no reason why you can't still enjoy it! Offer to have it at your home so the bride can relax and enjoy herself without the pressure of hosting. Some fluffy slippers and pyjamas would make a nice gift for the bride – even better if you can get wedding-themed ones. Or you could buy matching fluffy socks for all the guests. Line up a few films – you can't go wrong with girlie classics like *Grease, Dirty Dancing* or *Mamma Mia* – and stock up on popcorn and treats. For drinks, you could ask everyone to bring a bottle, or why not put a grown-up twist on a childhood favourite and make an enormous vat of Bailey's hot chocolate?

Kitchen Party: This is an old Irish tradition especially popular in the Cork area. It's hosted by the bride's mother or another older female relative such as an aunt, granny or older sister. Female friends and relatives of the bride are invited, along with her mum's friends, and her friends' mums!

Everyone brings small gifts for the bride to stock her kitchen. In the past, the idea was to set her up for married life with all she would need; nowadays the focus is more on fun gifts, but there's no reason why they can't be useful too. It's a good idea to set a spending limit, say €10.

If the bride would rather not have her mother-in-law watch her knocking back tequila slammers at the hen party, then a kitchen party is the ideal way to include her in the festivities. It can be an addition to the main hen party, or an alternative, if hen parties are really not her thing.

Potluck Dinner: This is an American tradition that has found its way across the Atlantic. Everyone brings a dish for the group to share. It's a great way to enjoy a dinner party without anyone being landed with the stress of cooking an entire meal for so many.

Decide if you are having a theme, e.g. Italian, Indian, and let people know a few weeks beforehand. Assign people to a different course or part of a course, and you can include as many different options as you think you might need – starter, main course, side veg or potatoes/rice, desserts, cheese and biscuits, chocolates.

You could offer to host to take the pressure off the bride. Even though everyone will be bringing something, there's still plenty to organise, like making sure you have enough clean dishes, glasses, cutlery and serving spoons, a hot oven to keep things warm, and of course getting the place ready and replenishing drinks all evening.

Sweaty Betties

If sitting around with cucumbers over her eyes or daintily sipping cups of tea in a posh hotel sounds like the bride's idea of hell, why not consider something more active? Head off to an adventure centre, or try go-karting, rock climbing or zip-lining. Book a hostel near some mountains, go off on a hike together and have a picnic at the summit. Try your hand at ice skating or skiing at an artificial slope. If you never got to try out a roller disco party as a child, why not do it now?

'For my sister's hen we headed to an outdoor pursuits centre. Half the hens signed up for off-road driving while the others, including my mam, did another activity. It was all going fine until we came to a sharp incline. I tried to brake and the brakes didn't work! Everyone was screaming and the car flipped over twice and landed upside down. I was suspended in my seat and couldn't get the seatbelt off, and my sister, the bride, wouldn't leave me. It felt like an eternity before they managed to get me out. I had some soft-tissue damage but my main concern was that my mam wouldn't find out. We all agreed to pretend that the off-road driving had been cancelled because of the weather!' *Louise, bridesmaid*

Crystal aMazing

If you love the idea of an organised activity but aren't the sporty types, there are other options. You could try an 'escape the room' challenge, where the hens have to work together to solve a series of clues. Or how about a CSI game, where the groom has been kidnapped and you have to follow clues to rescue him?

You could consider a class of some kind: a sewing class (to make fascinators to wear for the wedding), an art class (life drawing of a handsome male model, anyone?), or a dance class where you could acquire new skills and show them off at the nightclub later.

'For my friend's hen party we all dressed up as grannies and the bride was a grandad. It was the best craic I ever had. We had a knitting lesson over afternoon tea all dressed up – it was hilarious!' *Judy, bridesmaid*

Total Eclipse

What better way to liven up a night out than to make fools of yourselves belting out songs by ABBA or the

Spice Girls? Some karaoke bars allow you to hire a private booth so you won't have any other witnesses to your attempts to murder the finest pop songs of the last century. You may even be able to combine it with a Japanese meal, for the perfect one-stop night out. And of course plenty of cocktails to loosen any inhibitions – and ensure your memory of your dreadful performance will be as hazy as possible.

The Great Outdoors

If you want to go away somewhere but need to keep costs down, how about camping? Tents strung with fairy lights and bunting, long walks through the countryside, a hearty pub lunch, and an evening sitting around a campfire toasting marshmallows, telling ghost stories, and playing truth or dare. Some of the group might have tents and camping equipment already (or be able to borrow it), so it could make for a very cheap weekend away.

Bear in mind that it's unlikely to be everyone's cup of tea, but if you choose your spot carefully, the less outdoorsy among you could always come along for the campfire fun and then slink off to their comfy beds and en suites in a nearby B&B.

'Having a hen close to home can be as much fun as going away. For my sister's we did a night in, takeaway and pampering for anyone who fancied it. As she lives by the sea, we hired a beach hut for the next day. We popped down that morning and decorated it (no plastic willies in sight) and had beach games and hot chocolate. Then we went out that night for a lovely meal and dancing. It was great, and didn't cost stacks of cash!' *Beth, bridesmaid*

So 'You'

The most memorable hens are those which are truly personal to the bride. Is she a massive Harry Potter fan? Does she devour Jane Austen novels? Can she sing all the words to *The Sound of Music*? This could give you the perfect theme to base her hen party around. It might work particularly well for a party at home, where you could decorate accordingly, come up with games based on the theme, and give everyone little party favours.

'Aisling loves Agatha Christie so we wrote a murder-mystery game based on her play *Black Coffee*. We rented a beautiful dining room in a hotel – it had high ceilings and coving, thick velvet curtains and a big fireplace. We gave people their character descriptions when they arrived and bought some props (cheap beads and headbands) to give an inter-war-era feel. While Poirot (aka the bride) was interviewing suspects, everyone else searched for clues around the room. We had afternoon tea, then we didn't leave that room until dinner. Everyone got so into character and had a great laugh.' *Jenny, bridesmaid*

His & Hers

A joint hen and stag is sometimes known as a 'sten' (well, it certainly works better than 'hag'). This is still fairly unusual in Ireland – after all, the idea behind the hen or stag party is to celebrate each of them as individuals and to wave goodbye to single life in style – but it does suit some couples, particularly if they have been together for a long time and their friends are interwoven.

You'll need to coordinate with the best man to

make it happen. This is one occasion when keeping things secret from the bride and groom is probably going to prove tricky, though there is always room for some small surprises on the day. To get things started, the four of you could meet for coffee to thrash out some ideas and come up with a plan to keep everyone happy.

You might want to consider separate daytime activities (golf for the lads, hike for the girls) and then get together in the evening for dinner. Or do it the other way around – a massive game of paintballing for the whole gang, then go your separate ways for dinner (and maybe meet up again later for drinks if you just can't stay away from each other).

Once you know what the bride and groom would like, divide up the jobs with the best man and make sure you know who's doing what.

'Young lovers seek perfection. Old lovers learn the art of sewing shreds together and of seeing beauty in a multiplicity of patches.'
— **How to Make an American Quilt**

SAMPLE HEN PARTY #1:
BEAUTIFUL BARCELONA

A two-night Spanish city break

Day One: Hit the beach for a spot of sunbathing, or try your hand at watersports.

Evening: Go for tapas, then sample the local nightlife.

Day Two: Have a spa treatment, take a stroll down Las Ramblas and visit the Picasso Museum (museupicasso.bcn.cat/en).

Evening: Take a salsa class and then dance the night away.

Alternatives: Go on a food tour of Seville; visit the Moulin Rouge in Paris; take a canal boat tour in Amsterdam.

SAMPLE HEN PARTY #2:
DESTINATION DONEGAL

A one-night stay in the northwest

Daytime: Try go-karting at Letterkenny Activity Centre*, zoom through the air on the zip-line, then go for a stroll along the beach at Rathmullan.

Evening: Head into Letterkenny to start the evening off with cocktails and dinner, then dance the night away in one of Ireland's coolest nightclubs.

Next morning: Recharge the batteries with a hearty brunch.

Alternatives: Dress up as servants and ladies of a bygone age at the Victorian Escapade* in Mullingar; cook up a storm at Ballyknocken Cookery School* in Wicklow; go for a sassy photo shoot with Boudoir Girls* in Galway.

SAMPLE HEN PARTY #3:
DUBLIN CAN BE HEAVEN

A day out in the capital

Morning: Stretch your brains at Escape Dublin* – can you work together to solve the clues?

Afternoon: Celebrate your escape with a delicious afternoon tea.

Evening: Posh cocktails to toast the bride in style.

Alternatives: Hire a private cinema such as Brooks Cinema* to watch the bride's favourite film; turn detective at Murder on the Menu*; try a yoga class or some holistic treatments at the Elbow Room*.

*See p117 for contact details

Adding that extra touch

Whether you're having the hen party at home, in a restaurant or at a far-flung venue, adding little extra touches can make it really special for the bride.

Gifts

It's certainly not essential to bring gifts for the bride, but if you want to, just make sure the other hens know about it. You could suggest something in keeping with the theme, if there is one, or just let people use their imaginations. Small, fun, slightly risqué presents are the name of the game!

Or everyone could bring something silly for the bride to wear, and introduce them gradually over the course of the night. She might start off with just the de rigueur net veil but end up wearing a sparkly tiara, hot-pink feather boa, light-up zog-a-bongs, strings of beads and a ra-ra skirt, and carrying a blow-up, scantily clad doll. Understated, you? Never.

Games

Whether you're staying in or hitting the town, games can break the ice among guests and get that party started. A scavenger hunt is fun, and quizzes based on the bride work well, as she's the focal point and the one person everyone knows.

'For the hen party dinner I printed out some teenage photos of the bride as placemats and delivered them to the restaurant beforehand. It went down a treat with the bride and created hilarity and bonding with the hens. It was a good talking point to break the ice for people who didn't know one another.' *Geraldine, bridesmaid*

'How well do you know the bride?'

Come up with your own multiple-choice quiz that seeks to establish who knows the bride best, including those skeletons in the closet. Here are some examples to get you started: Why did the bride throw a tantrum at her tenth birthday party? Who did she kiss during freshers' week in college? What was her first summer job?

Rope in some help to make the questions as varied as possible. If your fellow bridesmaids know more about the bride's childhood, for example, then you might ask them to come up with a few from back then.

Mr and Mrs Quiz

For this you'll need to quiz the groom-to-be in advance! Come up with a list of questions, maybe ten about him and ten about her. Then on the hen

HENS UNPLUGGED!

Would the bride prefer not to have any photos of the hen night on social media? If so, a gentle reminder to people not to post any or tag her would be in order. No one needs their boss or their future mother-in-law to see them in the type of compromising positions some innocent hens find themselves in … and no one wants to risk offending someone who might feel they should have been invited! You can always share your photos with each other afterwards using whatever private messaging method you used to make the plans.

night the bride has to answer the same questions, and see how well they know each other. You could even record his answers and play them back after each of hers.

For example, where did they first kiss? Who was his last girlfriend before he met her? What is his most annoying habit? What would she bring to a desert island? Who is his best friend?

To make this quiz more interesting (and increase the chances of someone having to be carried out of the venue …) you could make it a shot-drinking game. If the bride gets a question wrong, she drinks a shot. If she gets one right, she nominates another hen to drink a shot. Just have a backup plan in case she keeps getting them wrong to the point of potential alcohol poisoning. Maybe her helpful bridesmaids can drink those extra shots for her!

Scavenger hunt

Divide the hens into teams and give them a list of items to find. You could include barmats from different pubs, a cocktail umbrella, a man's business card, a selfie with a stag party, a shot glass (not that we're advocating petty theft …). Agree a rendezvous point and the first group to return with all the items wins.

On the day of the hen

You'll need all your bridesmaid skills here – being organised with timekeeping, bills and transport arrangements; being friendly and welcoming and putting everyone at ease; and most of all, being the sparkling party person who helps keep the momentum going as the day and night unfolds.

As the hen-hostess with the hen-mostest, you'll need to keep a clear head, so go easy on the booze at least until the later part of the evening. You'll have quite a lot to think about, with staying on schedule if there are different events planned, sorting out the bills, and making sure the bride is being looked after. And try not to let the bride go overboard either. She wants to have a fabulous night or weekend that she'll always remember, not to pass out on the floor in a drunken coma.

See our Hen Party Countdown on p114 for a breakdown of what to do in the weeks and months running up to the big event!

'You'll always be my friend – you know too much.'
— Source unknown

CHAPTER FOUR

Bridesmaid Dilemmas

With any luck, all the wedding plans will go smoothly and everything will be sunshine and flowers between you and the bride. But issues do sometimes crop up, so let's have a look at some of the most common dilemmas bridesmaids find themselves facing – and how you can resolve them.

The bride says she doesn't want a hen party.

So you've been planning this from the moment the bride asked you to be her bridesmaid. You've researched the venues, you've got all her friends' numbers in your phone, you've even bought the willy straws and feather boas. Then the bride tells you she doesn't want a hen party. What's a girl to do?

First things first – find out why.

Is she worried about all the extra planning that's involved and just can't face it on top of planning the wedding? In that case, just reassure her that you're happy to handle everything, and all she has to do is turn up. And stick to this – don't go rushing back to her five minutes later to ask whether she wants to start the evening off with prosecco or cocktails. You're in charge. Make the call.

Does she hate the idea of a typical hen party – the screeching masses of girls in sky-high heels, the cheap net veils and L-plates, the enforced jollity of games filled with sexual innuendo? Reassure her that you know her likes and dislikes and that it will be in keeping with her tastes. If she's still feeling anxious, forget about making it a surprise and tell her exactly what you've got planned.

Is she reluctant to put her friends to the extra expense of a hen party, when they're already forking out a month's wages on travel and accommodation costs for the wedding itself, not to mention new outfits, hairdos and gifts? Is she afraid it's wedding overload – particularly since at a certain age we all find ourselves being invited to several weddings a year? If you think her concern is well founded, there are plenty of budget options for hens which will keep costs to a minimum (see the kitchen party, slumber party and potluck dinner mentioned in the previous chapter).

Is she concerned that her friends from various parts of her life won't gel together as a group? Again, this is something that can be solved by choosing the right type of hen party. A guided activity such as a dance class or an escape-the-room challenge takes away the pressure to make conversation and still allows the bride to celebrate with all the important females in her life.

Does she hate being the centre of attention and dread the thought of a fuss being made of her? For this sort of bride, the best thing to do is to keep things small. Forget the huge group – how about a simple celebration with just her bridesmaids? A spa day, afternoon tea or dinner, or just a takeaway and a movie? You don't even have to call it a hen party, but just persuade her that you would really love to mark the end of her singlehood with a little celebration for the girls. How could she say no?

If none of these reasons apply and she genuinely does not want a hen in any shape or form, then you'll have to respect her wishes. And hey, it's one less thing for you to worry about. Don't, whatever you do, decide to ignore her and throw her a surprise party complete with male stripper. She may never forgive you.

> *'A sister is a little bit of childhood*
> *that can never be lost.'*
> — *Marion Garretty*

You've got a new boyfriend. Should you bring him to the wedding?

First of all, how new is new? If we're talking someone you only started going out with a week before the wedding, then the answer is no. He won't be on the guest list, and it would be very unfair to ask the bride for an invitation. You don't want to be THAT bridesmaid. If, on the other hand, it's a month or two before the wedding and the bride and groom have made it clear that you're welcome to bring him, it's a bit more of a dilemma. Being a bridesmaid can be a pretty full-on job. You're going to be at the bride's beck and call all day, so you're not going to have a lot of time to spend with him.

Will he know other people at the wedding? If so, he'll have someone to talk to during the meal and at other points in the day when you're busy with your bridesmaid duties, and the two of you can look forward to a dance and a chat later.

But if he has no connection with the wedding other than through you, you might be better off leaving him at home this time. You'll have enough to do without needing to babysit him too.

'I had been going out with my new man for about six weeks before I was bridesmaid at my best friend's wedding. My friend tried to get me to invite him, but I said no – I wanted to be able to concentrate on being a bridesmaid without having to worry about him. I didn't even tell my boyfriend he was invited – he only found out years later!' *Emma, bridesmaid*

You find out you're pregnant. When should you tell the bride?

Congratulations! You might have hoped to keep your pregnancy a secret until the traditional three-month mark, but do consider telling the bride sooner as it's bound to affect her plans. If she's a close enough friend that she's asked you to be her bridesmaid, you can surely trust her with this exciting news. But whatever you do, make sure you tell her before there's any chance she will hear it from someone else – and do it in person if at all possible.

This is such an exciting time in your life; hopefully the bride will realise this and feel nothing but happiness for you. But as we all know, some brides have a tendency to be rather self-absorbed, imagining their wedding to be the centre of everyone's world and not just their own. Luckily this is usually a temporary condition, and they will come out the other side with their sense of perspective somewhat restored! But if this sounds like your bride, do choose your moment to tell her carefully. In the fitting room of a bridal boutique, as she tries to persuade you to go for a skintight bridesmaid dress she has set her heart on, is not that moment.

Lots of different dress styles will suit pregnant bridesmaids, but empire line (with a fitted bodice ending just below the bust and a long, flowing skirt below) is an ideal choice – many bridesmaid dresses come in this style anyway, and it will look good on the other bridesmaids too if the bride wants you all dressed the same. An empire silhouette has a timeless elegance that will enhance any wedding photos. Think Jane Austen's *Pride and Prejudice* for inspiration.

If your due date falls within a few weeks of the wedding, you may have no choice but to step down as bridesmaid. Sure, the baby could be late – or it could be a few weeks old by the wedding day and quite content to be brought along as an extra cute accessory – but given that they are unpredictable creatures, you can't guarantee that you will actually be able to make

'A successful marriage requires falling in love many times, always with the same person.'
— *Mignon McLaughlin*

it to the wedding. You don't need that stress, and the bride certainly doesn't.

Why not volunteer for a less high-profile role than bridesmaid so you can stay involved? For example, you could do a reading at the ceremony. That way, if you're suddenly unavailable on the day, someone else can step in.

If, on the other hand, the baby will be a couple of months old by the time the wedding rolls around, then you *should* be able to be a bridesmaid. It's fine to let the bride know that you would like to bring the baby to the wedding. If she doesn't have children herself it may not have occurred to her that it will be hard for you to leave the baby, but hopefully she will understand.

While some couples would prefer a child-free wedding, the motivation for this is usually numbers and/or the potential for noise and chaos. A small baby won't need a meal or a place setting and is fairly unlikely to go running down the aisle screaming and throwing things. As long as your partner is prepared to take the baby out if he or she starts crying during the ceremony or speeches, then the likelihood of any disruption is pretty minimal.

Bear in mind that you might need a dress that works for breastfeeding – something with a separate bodice and skirt should work. You don't want to have to disappear upstairs to your room every time the baby needs a feed.

'When I told my sister-in-law I was pregnant, I could see the look of panic on her face even as she was congratulating me. A couple of snide remarks over the next few weeks led me to believe that she really thought I should have waited until after her wedding. It didn't help that the dressmaker then asked me what size I would be in three months' time. How was I supposed to know?! Luckily another bridesmaid stepped in and suggested changing the style of our dresses to accommodate my expanding bump.' *Megan, bridesmaid*

Should you bring your older children to the wedding?

What about bringing your non-babies to the wedding? This may be academic if they are not invited. If it hasn't come up in conversation and their names are not on the invitation, then it's safe to assume they're not on the guest list. If this is the case, you really shouldn't ask if you can bring them along, as you'll be putting the bride in a pretty awkward position.

However, assuming the bride and groom HAVE told you your children are welcome, you might still be wondering if it's a good idea. Maybe you could concentrate better on your bridesmaid duties without the distraction of having them around. It could be a nice day off from your responsibilities, giving you the chance to really enjoy some grown-up time without having to worry about your little people – not to mention being able to party on into the night.

If it's a family wedding then it would be unusual not to bring your children. Imagine looking at the photos years later and having to explain to your little darling why you didn't want them to be there. The same goes for a very close friend who's regularly involved in your child's life.

If on the other hand the children don't know the bride and groom well (or are too young to care), then you may be better off leaving them at home. They'll probably have a lot more fun with a grandparent or aunt or uncle anyway.

If you do bring them, plan ahead. How will you keep them entertained during the day? Depending on their ages, colouring books and a few toys (not noisy ones) might help keep them occupied. Think about when would be a good point in the day for them to run off some steam outside somewhere – maybe while the photos are being taken, or before the meal, or both. If they are fussy eaters, find out what the hotel menu is like and plan accordingly. Will they manage a late night, or will there be hell to pay if they're kept up past their usual bedtime? The hotel may be able to recommend a babysitter who can sit in the room with them for a few hours so both parents can continue to enjoy the party.

'My sister wanted a child-free wedding, but she said that of course this didn't apply to her nieces and nephews. My daughters loved being a part of her big day and had so much fun with their cousins.' *Natalie, bridesmaid*

You live far away from the bride. How can you stay involved?

You and the bride are living in different towns, or maybe even different countries. And the wedding may well be in a third location. Can you really do much to help her with the practicalities?

The short answer is yes. Modern communication is your friend. Imagine being a bridesmaid back when you had to send your dress measurements in the post, or when a long-distance phone call cost a small fortune. (On the other hand, maybe brides' expectations were a little lower back then …) Instead you'll be able to stay in the loop with group chats on WhatsApp, see the bride's moodboard on Pinterest, or tag her in bridal tips on Facebook.

Even organising the hen party can be done from a distance. You can do so much research online, and read reviews of venues and suppliers. Of course, if there's something special that needs to be checked out in person, maybe another bridesmaid could take care of that – or the bride herself if it's not a surprise. But you can still do the booking over the phone and be the contact person who coordinates all those schedules.

Use Skype/FaceTime/video chat to catch up with the bride. It'll make you feel more connected, and you can model your dresses for each other and have a giggle almost as if you're in the same room.

Having to travel home separately for the hen party and the wedding might put a strain on your finances – as well as your career and family life. See if there's a way around this. Could the hen party be held closer to the wedding than usual, say the week before, so you can make it part of the same trip? Or if you can't make the main hen party, could you have a second, more low-key one in the days before the wedding – maybe involving a spa visit or something equally relaxing?

If you live close enough to make two separate trips, try to set a date for the hen as early as possible so you're not booking expensive flights at the last minute. But if you know it's just not going to be possible for you to attend, be sure to let the bride know well in advance so she's not too disappointed. She knew where you lived when she asked you to be bridesmaid, so she must have realised some things would be difficult for you. You'll still be there to hold her hand from afar, and her bouquet on the big day.

> *'If there ever comes a day when we can't be together, keep me in your heart, I'll stay there forever.'*
> — *AA Milne*, Winnie the Pooh

The bride has turned into a total Bridczilla!

We've all heard the horror stories of brides who are obsessed to the point where they can't talk about anything else except the wedding and are making utterly unreasonable demands of those around them. This is the extreme end of the scale, but could your bride be heading in that direction – and what can you do to pull her back from the brink?

It's OK for brides to become a little self-centred. It might be your turn one day – or maybe it already has been, and your friends are still speaking to you. (What do you mean you never once overreacted to some minor wedding issue? Are you sure everyone around you would back you up on this?)

Try to remember that planning a wedding is a very

stressful time. The bride will be feeling a lot of pressure to have everything perfect, and the responsibility can be so overwhelming that a normally rational person can go a tiny bit crazy. Be the calm presence she needs right now, reassuring her that everything will be fine and that her plans sound wonderful.

Rest assured that the friend you know and love is in there somewhere and will re-emerge after the wedding ready to be there for you once more, and to talk about things other than cakes and flowers. In the meantime, smile and nod and allow your mind to wander as much as you can get away with.

Offer her a shoulder to cry on when she needs it, and a glass of wine or a giant box of chocolates to counteract the stress. (Don't forget to indulge in the same yourself; it sounds like you've earned it.) Take her mind off the wedding with a night out or give her a voucher for a relaxing massage.

'Those who bring sunshine to the lives of others cannot keep it from themselves.'
— *J.M. Barrie*

If her demands are getting too much for you, take a deep breath and remind yourself that being a bridesmaid is not a full-time job. You have a life of your own to think about, and while it's nice to help out where you can, this shouldn't be at the expense of your job, social life – or sanity.

Tell the bride that you're feeling a bit overwhelmed with all she's asked you to take on, and that you're not going to be able to manage it all. Ask her which of the responsibilities is most important to her and say you'll take care of those. See if you can split the jobs with the other bridesmaids, or put them back on the bride. She may decide that sourcing the exact shade of napkins to match her bouquet isn't that important if she has to take care of it herself.

Stop responding instantly when she calls or texts. Leave it until you have the time. She should soon get the message that your life doesn't totally revolve around her wedding.

Don't be tempted to get into a bitchfest with the other bridesmaids about Bridezilla's behaviour. Yes, they may well be going through the same trauma as you, but moaning about the bride behind her back is just going to create a nasty atmosphere in the run-up to the wedding. If you really need to vent, choose someone a little more removed from the situation.

And don't forget, this will all be finished soon; once the wedding day is over she will go back to being her old self, perhaps even feeling a bit sheepish about how over-the-top she was. You can hang up your bridesmaid shoes and breathe a sigh of relief. (And then start plotting how you'll get your own back when your wedding comes around.)

'My sister-in-law's wedding was abroad and we were already paying €3,000 for flights and accommodation. Then she wanted me to pay €300 for a dress for my six-year-old and another €400 to hire a suit for my four-year-old. I sent her a link to Dunnes instead.' *Rhona, bridesmaid*

CHAPTER FIVE

~ The Wedding Build-up ~

he hen party is done and dusted, and you can be proud of how well everything went (or maybe you're just glad it's all over). Don't get too relaxed now – the wedding day is fast approaching, and you've still got plenty of bridesmaid duties to see to.

The weeks before the wedding

If the wedding is out of town, don't forget to **book your accommodation** for the night before and night of the wedding (and maybe an extra day or two either side, if you really want to make an occasion of it!). Don't assume the bride and groom will have booked a room for you – ask. Even if they have made the booking for you, don't assume that they are going to pay for it. It's not usually the done thing, unless you're a struggling student and they've just won the lottery. After all, you would be paying for your hotel room even if you were just attending the wedding as a guest.

Remember to make time for your own **dress fittings**, if needed, and any **beauty treatments** you need in the days before the wedding. Check with the bride in case she has plans for you to get your nails done together!

The last few weeks before the wedding will be a very busy time for the bride. No matter how well organised she is, there are lots of jobs that can't be done until close to the time. Collecting dresses, making appointments, confirming details with suppliers, and the inevitable stress of trying to finalise guest numbers when some people have failed to RSVP on time. Can you take some of the stress away by **helping with the wedding to-do list**? For example, you could arrange hair and beauty appointments for all the bridal party. Or if some of the annoying non-RSVPers are people you know, you could be the one to chase them up.

She might also need some practical help, such as **making up favours**, or sorting out the **wedding booklets** or **decorations** for the reception. Turn this into a fun night in – nothing like a bottle of bubbly and a few nibbles to make threading ribbons or stapling paper seem more fun than chore.

BEST BRIDESMAID EVER

Sometimes the best thing you can do for the bride is to take her mind off the wedding completely. Arrange to go and see a film together, go shopping for clothes for her honeymoon (that doesn't count as wedding stress!), or let your hair down with a mad night out. This is a good way to remind her that there is more to life than her wedding (but please, don't actually say that out loud. At least not to her).

One week before the wedding

Go to the bride's **dress fitting**, if you can, and take the opportunity to ask the shop assistant or dressmaker for tips. For example, what's the best way to remove stains from the dress if something happens on the day? And if the dress has a train, make sure you know how to pin it up for when the dancing starts.

Try on your whole outfit. Make sure your dress fits and that you have everything you need. **Wear your shoes** around the house to break them in.

'My bridesmaid told me three days before the wedding that her dress didn't fit. She'd been working up to tell me for weeks! Luckily she was my only bridesmaid so we just went out shopping for another one – but I could have done without the stress so close to the wedding!'
Lucy, bride

This is a good time to put together a kit of **emergency supplies** the bride and bridesmaids might need on the day. (See p119.) Obviously, it will rather spoil the bridesmaid look if you're carrying this stuff in an enormous rucksack, so plan to stash it somewhere – in someone's car if possible, or at a suitable place at the reception venue.

Ask the bride if there's **anything you can help with** this week. Even if she prefers to look after the arrangements herself, she will appreciate your interest and concern.

The day before the wedding

The big day is nearly here! The day before is a good time for **manicures and pedicures** to make sure they're pristine for the wedding day.

The bride and groom will probably have lots of last-minute jobs like dropping off wedding **booklets** at the church or ceremony venue, collecting the **cake** and bringing **decorations** and favours to the hotel. See if there's anything you can help out with to take the pressure off.

Check you have everything you need in the **emergency kit**. Make sure you know the **schedule** for the next day. What time is your hair appointment? How long will you have afterwards for getting ready? What time do you need to leave for the ceremony? If you're doing a reading, print it or write it out on nice paper. If you're making a speech, have a run through it and make sure you have your notes ready.

The rehearsal

If the couple are having a church service, the rehearsal often takes place the evening before the wedding, to ensure that everyone's in town and all the details are fresh in people's minds for the next day. The bride and groom, bridesmaids, best man and groomsmen need to attend, and possibly people doing the readings too. It's basically just a **run-through** of the ceremony so everyone knows what they need to do and where they need to be at each stage.

The American tradition of the '**rehearsal dinner**' has become popular in Ireland, but without the formalities of speeches and toasts. It usually involves the bridal party and immediate families of the bride and groom having a meal together – a nice chance for them to get to know each other a little bit, if they haven't already, plus it saves everyone from having to cook! If the bride hasn't mentioned it, check whether

*'Love is composed of a single soul
inhabiting two bodies.'*
— *Aristotle*

anything is happening. It's usually a casual affair and you will probably be more than welcome to bring your other half along.

The evening before

Tradition dictates that after midnight the bride and groom don't see each other until the wedding ceremony, and the bride spends the evening with her bridesmaids. Most couples still keep up this custom. Try to get home at a sensible time so you and the bride can both get a **good night's sleep**. And don't pester her with trivial things – she needs her beauty sleep!

It's a good idea to **wash your hair** the night before – if you leave it until the morning of the wedding it makes it trickier for the hairdresser to work with.

'It was midnight on the night before my wedding and I was about to go to sleep when my bridesmaid came into my room demanding that I help her glue on her nails. Then she acted like it was my fault when her ancient nail glue wouldn't work!' *Carol, bride*

CHAPTER SIX

The Wedding Day

All those months of preparations, dress fittings, hen parties and celebrations have been building up to this. The big day is finally here. A day filled with love and laughter and of course the odd stressful moment too, as even the most laidback bride may find herself succumbing to nerves. But she needn't worry, as you'll be right there by her side through it all. Here's what you can expect as the day unfolds.

MORNING

Big hair, don't care

Wedding days start early. The ceremony might not be on until 2pm, but there's a good chance the bride has made **hair appointments** for 9am – if not earlier. This might seem excessive to you, but with several people to get their hair done, then **make-up** to fit in after that, the time will soon fly by. Whatever you do, don't be late. The last thing you want is to start the day off on a stressful note. Wear a shirt or a **top with a wide neck** so it won't be a problem to pull it over your head after you've had your hair done.

The bride might have a particular hairstyle in mind for all her bridesmaids, but if she's leaving it up to you it's a good idea to **bring a photo** of a hairstyle you like – something from a magazine or website, or better still a photo of your own hairstyle from a different event. It's a lot easier to show the hairdresser a photo than to try to describe it. Don't be tempted to try any wild experiments or to go against the bride's wishes.

'I paid for all my bridesmaids to have their hair done in natural-looking waves. When we got back to the hotel where we were getting dressed, they all disappeared into another room and straightened their hair without telling me! I wasn't impressed.' *Sharon, bride*

Wedding fuel

Don't forget to eat! And see that the bride does too – no one wants her fainting as she walks down the aisle. Make sure there's enough time after the hair appointments for you to fit in a **decent breakfast**. And **brush your teeth** before you get your make-up done.

Making up is hard to do

If you have a make-up artist coming to prettify you all, know what you want – again, a **photo** can be a good idea, or just be prepared to say 'I like a natural look' or 'I want to emphasise my eyes'. And remember that now is not the time to try anything too dramatic.

If you're doing your own make-up, give yourself **plenty of time** and have **wipes** on hand for quick fixes. Get yourself dressed nice and early. Remember that you need to be **on hand to help the bride** get ready, and that she may have a **photographer** coming for those 'getting ready shots'.

'My bridesmaid turned into an utter diva on the morning of the wedding, demanding heavy eyeliner and dark eyeshadow. The make-up artist refused as she knew I wanted a more natural look. The bridesmaid locked herself in the bathroom and cried for an hour.'

Niamh, bride

Meringue time

Allow enough time to help the bride into her finery! **Wedding dresses** can be complicated affairs – so many hooks and buttons, and that's before you start arranging the veil. Have a **practice run** beforehand if you can so you know what to expect. Much better to be sitting down relaxing while you wait for the car to arrive than running around frantically searching for a needle and thread while the chauffeur looks at his watch.

'I realised on the morning of my friend's wedding that my dress didn't fit. It had been fine at the fitting two weeks before. My husband managed to just about get the zip up, but I could barely breathe – it was awful! As soon as the ceremony, photos and meal were done I had to change. I found out the next day I was pregnant!'

Sally, bridesmaid

Chill pills

Make the getting-ready bit of the day **fun** for the bride. One of the reasons she chose you as her bridesmaid is because she knew you'd have a laugh together at this very moment. A **bottle of champagne** can set a suitably celebratory note, but stick to half a glass at most – you don't want to be bursting for the loo or looking glassy-eyed as you walk down the aisle.

If she is getting stressed, be the calm, **reassuring** presence she needs (you can keep this up for one more day!). Don't go straight to her with any problems that arise. Sort it out yourself if you can, or speak to someone else in the wedding party.

'My mum got nail polish on my sister's wedding dress half an hour before she put it on. The other bridesmaids and I kept her occupied while we lovingly and slowly removed it. It was fine and we never told her until weeks later!'
Sue, bridesmaid

Flower power

The **flowers** are usually delivered on the morning

– **bride's bouquet, bridesmaids' bouquets** and **corsages** for the mothers. If the **buttonholes** for the groom and his attendants are not being delivered separately you may have to arrange to get them to wherever the groom is getting ready.

Late late show

As the morning goes on, keep an eye on the **time**. It's traditional for brides to be a little late for the ceremony – but only a little. Any more than fifteen minutes risks being seen as rude to the guests, and for certain venues, it may cause serious pressure, if there is another ceremony following after yours. Avoid delays by knowing what you should be doing at each stage of the morning and giving the bride a gentle nudge if you think she's falling behind **schedule**.

'I don't want someone who promises me the world.
I just want someone to sit on the porch with me and
watch it go by as we grow old together.'
— **Up**

BEST BRIDESMAID EVER

Does the bride have her something old, new, borrowed and blue? If she has forgotten, can you lend it to her? A ring could be both old and borrowed. For an emergency 'something blue', a toenail painted blue will do the trick (assuming she isn't wearing sandals!).

'My bridesmaid was never there when I needed her. She missed the rehearsal but showed up in time for dinner. She demanded to go first at the hairdresser's, then told me she wouldn't wear the very expensive shoes she'd picked out herself and got me to pay for. After the photographs we went for sandwiches and while my husband and I were getting some extra photos taken, she and her boyfriend ate ours as well as their own as she said she thought we'd be too excited to eat. I was starving, but my lovely flower girl came to the rescue – she'd saved me two squares of chocolate! I barely saw my bridesmaid after that. She went home the next day and even though I tried to get in touch with her, I've never seen her again.' *Aoife, bride*

CEREMONY

Outside the ceremony venue, arrange the bride's **veil and train**. Give her a quick scan to make sure everything is perfect, and ask another bridesmaid to do the same for you! If you've got a **handbag** or anything else with you, ask someone to mind it for you – you should only be carrying your flowers during the ceremony.

The usual order for walking down the aisle is **flower girls first**, then **bridesmaids** one by one, with the **chief bridesmaid last**, and then finally the **bride and her escort** (traditionally her father, but now often both parents). If you're doing something different, this will have been covered in the rehearsal.

The **music** should give you your cue to go. Walk slowly and remember to smile.

If you're looking after the **groom's ring** during the ceremony, your thumb is a good place to keep it safe! But often the best man will look after both rings.

If there are **flower girls and page boys**, keep an eye on them during the ceremony, as their parents may be seated too far away to be able to step in quickly.

The bridesmaids stand with the bride and groom while they make their **vows**. One of the best bits about being a bridesmaid is being close enough to see their faces at this moment, so do savour it.

After the ceremony the chief bridesmaid and the best man **sign the register** as witnesses to the marriage. The bride and groom walk back up the aisle, followed by the chief bridesmaid and best man, and then any other bridesmaids and groomsmen in pairs. The entire bridal party (that includes you) then **waits outside** to greet other guests as they leave.

For Catholic couples, it was traditional that the best man and chief bridesmaid would be godparents to the couple's first child. So do try to get on with the best man if there's a chance you're going to be looking at him again over a christening font!

PHOTOS

Formal photos of the wedding party and families are usually taken **outside** the church or venue. Bridesmaids can play a role here in **rounding up** the right people! Afterwards the bridal party may go elsewhere to take some **special photos**, while the other guests proceed to the reception venue. Some tips for looking your best in the wedding photos:

- Top up your face powder frequently to avoid that shiny look.
- Turn your hips slightly to the side to give a slimmer silhouette.
- Keep your chin up to avoid looking jowly.
- Look away between photos for a more natural smile.
- Don't say 'cheese', say 'money'!

RECEPTION

The **drinks reception** will probably be well underway by the time the bridal party arrive after taking the photos. Hopefully someone has saved a glass of bubbly for you! This is a good time to **mingle** with other guests and especially to speak to any older relatives (particularly important if you're related to the bride and they're your relatives too!). Small talk is the name of the game. Have some conversation-starters in mind if you're naturally shy. There's always that good old Irish reliable, the weather. 'Isn't it a perfect day for a wedding?' or 'What a shame about the rain, but nothing could spoil this day' – delete as appropriate.

Having a way to escape a dull conversation is a good plan too. Luckily as bridesmaid you have the perfect get-out line: 'Could you excuse me, I just need to check if the bride needs anything.' Who's going to argue with that?

DINNER

You may need to help the bride **remove her veil** before dinner. This is a good opportunity to touch up **make-up** too.

The hotel staff will announce dinner and ask guests

to take their seats. The rest of the bridal party take their places, while the bride and groom are last to enter. Their **names are announced** and they enter the room to a **standing ovation**.

The bridal party normally sit at the **top table** – bride, groom, bridesmaids, best man, groomsmen, bride's parents, groom's parents, and the priest or minister if it was a church wedding. If there are flower girls and page boys, they don't usually sit at the top table; neither do partners of the bridal party.

SPEECHES

You might have thought you were off the hook when it came to speeches – but think again. Traditionally the only speeches given at the wedding dinner were by the **groom**, the **best man** and the **bride's father**. But times they are a-changing, and quite right too – there aren't

'It is only with the heart that one can see rightly;
what is essential is invisible to the eye.'
— Antoine de Saint-Exupéry, The Little Prince

many other spheres of life where the modern woman is willing to sit back and let a man speak for her! So be prepared for the fact that the bride might ask you to **say a few words.** Keep it short and sweet, and don't feel obliged to try to copy the best man in coming up with outrageous stories from the bride's past. Just a few words about what a lovely person she is, how much it means to you to be a part of her special day, and how happy you are for the newlywed couple is enough.

'I was chief bridesmaid for my sister and she asked if I'd like to say a few words. I decided to write a poem for her and her new husband. It went down very well with the guests – apart from the fact that I started crying halfway through! When I got married a few years later, my sister surprised me by reading the same poem.'
Áine, bridesmaid

If you're struggling for inspiration, try one of these:
- Read a quote about love and marriage
- Tell the story of how the bride and groom met

- Mention a friend who couldn't be at the wedding but is thinking of the happy couple
- Describe something funny that happened at the hen party (nothing too risqué!)
- Share a childhood memory about the bride (if you're sisters or old friends) or how you first got to know each other

'My bridesmaid wrote her speech in the form of a letter to me, including lots of memories, since we've been friends for a long time. It was lovely, and she gave it to me to keep afterwards.' *Nicola, bride*

DANCING

The meal is done, the speeches are over – you're almost off duty. Almost, but not quite. The bride and groom will have their **first dance**, and then for the **second dance** the bridal party take to the floor too – this can even happen halfway through the first dance, if the bride and groom prefer not to have all the focus on them! **Pair up** with the same **attendant** you walked up the aisle with – chief bridesmaid with best man, bridesmaid with groomsman and so on.

At last the formal part of the day is done. You can relax and enjoy the rest of the night.

How to be a help to the bride:

- Make sure she has a **drink** – brides won't be carrying cash and can end up being forgotten or losing their drinks as they mingle. Bring her **water** too so she doesn't get dehydrated.

- Be available to **field questions** from the hotel staff or other suppliers like the DJ or photographer over the evening.

- Are people out dancing? Maybe the evening hasn't really got going yet or the music is a bit of a let-down, but the bride and groom won't be happy to see the dancefloor empty. Have a word with the band or DJ and **suggest some tunes** you know will get the crowd going. Encourage people to **get out there and dance** – and show a good example by doing so yourself!

- Collect some **souvenirs** for the bride – table decorations, menu, placenames. She'll be too busy to think of doing this herself, but she'll love to have them afterwards.

THE DAY AFTER

Don't switch off just yet! Your bridesmaid duties are not quite over. The day after the wedding, the bride and groom may have a **special event** planned – brunch, a barbecue, drinks – and unless you have a *really* good excuse (being hungover doesn't count) you should be there. Hopefully, though, there won't be too much for you to do besides show up, and you can be pretty sure the bride won't need you to adjust her veil.

Remember to tell the **bride's parents** (or whoever hosted the wedding) how much you enjoyed the day and that you were delighted to be a part of it.

As the bride and groom head off on their **honey-moon**, there are some **post-wedding jobs** you could help the bride out with. Her dress will need to be taken to the **dry cleaner**. Her mother may well be looking after this, but it would be nice to offer. They might have **wedding presents** of cash or cheques that you could lodge in the bank for them.

Plan something nice for yourself for after the wedding. Take an extra day or two off work and go away for a night, or stay at home and do absolutely nothing. You've earned a **lazy day** or two!

'Being a bridesmaid is a lot of work on the day. Just keeping an eye on the bride, making sure she's calm going into the ceremony, that she has everything for the photos, and so on, really keeps you on your toes, and until the first dance is done you don't feel like you're off duty. Not that I want to sound like I'm giving out! It was a brilliant day, but the one heads-up that I'd want to give other bridesmaids is how busy a day it is, so give yourself a few days off afterwards to recover!' *Laura, bridesmaid*

BEST BRIDESMAID EVER

While they are on their honeymoon, get some wedding photos printed for them. It will be at least a few weeks before the wedding photographer has their album ready, and in the meantime they will love to have a few snapshots they can show colleagues and friends. Even if there are dozens of photos up on social media, nothing beats having physical copies you can coo over together.

~ Bridesmaid Countdown ~

Six months to one year to go

- Help the bride shop for her wedding dress
- Meet up with the other bridesmaids
- Go shopping for the bridesmaid dresses
- Start planning the hen party (see: Hen Party Countdown)
- Book accommodation for the wedding

Four months to go

- Buy shoes and other accessories
- Make hen party bookings (see: Hen Party Countdown)

Three months to go

- Make hair and beauty appointments (if the bride isn't looking after this herself)

One month to go

- Have dress fittings

- Hold hen party
- Break in shoes
- Start planning your speech, if you're making one

One week to go
- Have final dress fitting
- Collect dress
- Make sure you have your complete outfit ready to go – dress, cover-up, shoes, accessories
- Put emergency kit together (see p119)
- Go over your speech
- Check if the bride needs your help with anything

Day before the wedding
- Go for a manicure and pedicure (with the bride if possible)
- Check that the bride has everything she needs
- Check your emergency kit
- Check your notes for your speech
- Attend the rehearsal
- Attend the rehearsal dinner
- Make sure the bride gets an early night

Hen Party Countdown

As early as you can
- Talk to the bride about what type of hen she would like
- Come up with a guest list
- Set a date
- Set up a social media group and ask other hens to save the date

Three months to go
- Discuss plans with the other bridesmaids
- Book the venue/restaurant/accommodation
- Book entertainers/activities/classes
- Let other hens know the plans

One month to go
- Divide the to-do list between the bridesmaids
- Shop for accessories, decorations, party favours, etc.
- Let hens know if there is anything they should

bring with them, e.g. novelty gifts, old photos of the bride, change of clothes for activities

- Let hens know how much everything will cost

One week to go

- Confirm the bookings
- Come up with any games or quizzes
- Finalise numbers (call anyone who hasn't RSVP'd)

Day before

- Remind hens of the meeting place and times. If some will be joining you later, give them a rough idea of where you'll be when, and make sure they have a mobile phone number for a bridesmaid (or preferably two)

⁓ Inspo and Resources ⁓

For more bridesmaid inspiration, check out these websites for information on venues and suppliers all over Ireland, fab photos of real-life weddings and discussion forums where you can find out what brides are really thinking!

www.onefabday.com

www.weddingsonline.ie

www.mrs2be.ie

www.confetti.ie

www.thevow.ie

Looking further afield, you'll find lots of ideas on:

www.stylemepretty.com

www.bridalmusings.com

www.brides.com

www.100layercake.com

www.youandyourwedding.co.uk

www.theknot.com

For tips on readings and speeches, check out:

www.hitched.ie

www.weddingspeechbuilder.com

For online bridesmaid dresses, try:

www.asos.com

www.bhldn.com

www.chichiclothing.com

www.mialondon.co.uk

For hen parties with a difference, check out:

www.lkactivitycentre.com

www.victorianescapade.com

www.ballyknocken.ie

www.boudoirgirls.net

www.escape-dublin.com

www.brookshotel.ie

www.murderonthemenu.ie

www.the-elbowroom.com

Budget Planner

Traditionally the bride and groom pay for the bridesmaid's dress and extras, hairdresser and make-up artist, while the bridesmaid pays for accommodation and so on herself, but here's the full list, just in case!

Items:	Estimated Cost €	Actual Cost €
Dress		
Shoes		
Lingerie		
Jewellery		
Hair		
Make-up		
Nails		
Hen party		
Accommodation		
Travel		
Wedding present		
Other		

Bridesmaid's Emergency Kit

- Make-up
- Lip balm
- Nail varnish to cover any chips
- Sun cream (for summer weddings)
- Tissues and cotton buds (for running mascara)
- Blotting paper
- Hairpins and hairspray
- Sanitary products
- Plasters (and blister plasters)
- Snacks and water
- Spare tights and clear nail vanish for fixing ladders
- Mini-sewing kit and safety pins
- Baby wipes (for getting stains off dresses, but do check that the fabric is suitable)
- Mints
- Painkillers
- Cash
- Phone charger
- Timeline for the day
- Contact details for everyone involved in the wedding

Notes

Also by Natasha Mac a'Bháird

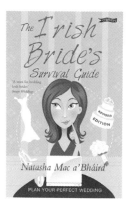

So you are getting married and you want the Big Day to be perfect? Well, look no further.

Based on her own wedding experience and the collected wisdom of other brides (and the odd groom), the author will take you through every stage of this happy process, from the proposal to the honeymoon.

* Who does what * Church & civil requirements * Rings and things * Dress to impress * Cakes, cars and photos * Hen parties to honeymoons * Budget Planner * * Countdown from engagement to 'I do' *

'Everything you need to know about making your wedding day one to remember.' *Sunday World*

'A must for budding Irish brides.' *Image Weddings*